TAKING DOMINION

THROUGH THE POWER OF

MIDNIGHT PRAYER

**What Every Christian Believer Must Know To
Stand Strong, Overcome And Successfully
Breakthrough In Their Christian Lives**

EMMANUEL KORANTENG

TABLE OF CONTENTS

INTRODUCTION

The purpose of this book is to awaken you spiritually to engage in prayer more than ever before. For many are the plans and satanic activities that are programmed against man in the earth realm. And they mostly occur at the midnight hour.

Staying awake at night to battle in prayer brings victory on every side and causes you to have success and dominion in every phase of your life.

Psalms 91:5

"Thou shalt not be afraid for the terror by night; nor for

the arrow that flieth by day;"

CHAPTER ONE

What are the benefits of prayer? Some good things you must experience in prayer with God;

Your relationship with God becomes very strong and tight.

Prayer means talking to God. Your continual prayer brings you closer to God than before. It causes your friendship and intimacy to be very strong

You become spiritually strong

Continual Prayer causes you to be stronger and more sensitive in the spirit. Anything that happens behind the scenes of your life becomes open to you when you often pray; you become a firebrand

Prayer makes you attract good things to your life

Good things are programmed on the path of those who pray. Prayer eliminates the occurrence of bad or evil happenings.

Prayer aborts the plans of the enemy against you.

Continual prayer disturbs the plans and plots set up by the enemy against your life. It makes them not succeed. You destroy their works and plans.

Prayer makes you dangerous in the spirit realm

When you often pray, you become very dangerous in the realms of the spirit. You take dominion over any region you find yourself in, and also become very powerful

CHAPTER TWO

What happens when you don't pray?

Prayer is therefore very helpful. A person who doesn't pray has certain happenings in his or her life. Below are the five things that happen when you don't pray;

When you don't pray;

Gods plan for your life does not come to pass.

Prayerlessness causes gods plan and purposes for your life not to manifest. Prayerless life delays your destiny. You abort the fulfillment of your life's destiny.

You become an empty vessel

Lack of prayer makes you empty in life, opening your life to demonic use and control. When you don't pray, demonic powers dictate and control how your life should go. They use you to do their plans and operations.

Good things do not happen to you.

Prayerlessness aborts good things that must happen for you. The blessings and good things God has for you are aborted by the enemy.

There is no progress in your life

Your lack of prayer stops your progress in life. Your goals, dreams, and aspirations come to a halt and are never achieved as you stop praying. The enemy places more obstacles in your way and hinders your progress.

God's power is absent in your life

A person who doesn't pray is denied of God's power. The manifestation of God's power, signs, miracles, and wonders are never seen. You become the mockery of people because good things do not happen for you. Most of your efforts

result in total failure.

CHAPTER THREE

How to pray for effective results

The presence of dirt in a place prevents access to good things. The presence of dirt in a person's environment generally denies good health in the person's life.

In the same way, dirt does not attract good things. Spiritually when it comes to prayer, the object or personality whom we engage with is God. And God dislikes dirt/impureness.

Therefore, to engage in prayer, you must be pure, clean in heart, hands and your whole life.

To begin prayer, practice the following;

Firstly, express gratefulness unto God.

Be grateful to God by showing appreciation and thanksgiving for His goodness and mercies upon your life.

Secondly, ask for forgiveness of sins

Do not pray without applying the word.

Equip yourself with scriptures related to your prayer requests.

God works through His word. Jesus overcame Satan through the word during his temptation in the wilderness. Prayer with scriptures is more powerful and avails much. Prayer without scriptures is empty and carries no power.

Stand on the word to pray always. Use the psalms to express thanksgiving in prayer.

Praying with the word means praying with God. For the word is God Himself. Do not pray emptied of the word. Every desire of the heart is accomplished when scripturally filled prayer is made. Soak your self with the scriptures daily for effective prayer results.

CHAPTER FOUR

The power of midnight prayer

What times do we pray? Prayer is necessary at all times. Prayer is necessary for the morning hours, prayer is necessary for the afternoon hours, and prayer is necessary for the evening and night hours. In fact, prayer is needed at all times. That is why Jesus stated that "men ought to pray and not faint". The scriptures encourage us to pray without ceasing.

However, the part of the day's cycle in which prayer is needed most is at midnight. The midnight phase is where the spiritual energies of man become low and the energies of the spiritual realm increase. At midnight the strength of the physical human body is low as a result of intense physical activity it goes through during the day and tends to relax to sleep at night. This makes the ability to yield the human body to prayer very difficult due to tiredness and tends to sleep.

The spiritual activity in the spiritual realm increases at midnight hour. At 12 midnight, we enter into another day (A.M).

At that period, the spiritual door into the new day is opened in the realm of the spirit. At that moment, satanic activity including demons, witchcraft agents, principalities and powers take to flight for satanic meetings to plan and operate mainly against humanity (especially Christian believers) on earth.

Demonic entities that inhabit water bodies do meet in the water realm, those that inhabit the air meet in the air realm. Those that inhabit in trees and rocks meet in those regions. They all meet in their specific regions mainly to plan and determine what must be done to suppress and overcome

Christian lives on the earth. We call this period of satanic activity the WITCH HOUR or THE DEVIL HOUR.

A strong Christian believer who is knowledgeable of such ongoing activity and stays awake at midnight will succeed by overcoming these forces in prayer. This calls for the necessity of midnight prayer at all levels of human life.

The life of the day begins at 12midnight into the break of dawn. The arrangement and planning of anything that must take place within the day of mankind in the physical realm are determined by spiritual forces at the hour of 12midnight to 3 am before the break of the morning. within this period, every witchcraft and satanic plan against man is determined and programmed into operation before morning.

Principalities and powers take over their planned activity and cause their manifestation in the earth realm. This is why weak and prayerless men fall prey to sicknesses, diseases, failure, disgrace, disappointment, accidents, death, poverty, and many more.

As a Christian, because 12midnight is the starting point of spiritual activity, it is best to stay awake early at 12am to pray than to begin your prayer at 3 am for effective results.

As they meet at 12midnight, you also arise and start an intensive prayer. Your prayer destroys the plans and operations they program during their meetings and by the time morning breaks forth, you are guaranteed to rule in dominion, victory, and success the whole day.

This is practically what takes place in the spiritual realm at midnight period; at midnight the great spiritual forces of God including the Holy Ghost and the host of angels are released to attend to all Christian believers, attending to their prayer and spiritual welfare. And so, any Christian who stays asleep and is not active in prayer at that period is devoid of spiritual reinforcement or backup by the Holy Spirit and angelic forces and becomes vulnerable to the attacks of the enemy.

On the other side, satanic forces including principalities, powers, and spiritual rulers in high places are also set into motion using their satanic human agents on the earth realm to accomplish their mission of destruction against Christians.

CONCLUSION

The midnight hours are one of the most powerful and yet most vital times to combat the enemy. The prayer said at 12 a.m. is known as midnight prayer. It's that time of year when the enemy gathers with their spells to fight their victims. At that hour, a wicked individual can rise and fire nasty arrows. People frequently have unpleasant dreams and spiritual attacks on their bodies around midnight. The midnight power is a battleground between believers and demons. Spiritual attacks are more common between the hours of 12 am and 3 am. Witchcraft powers, marine powers, household powers, strongmen, witch doctors, and other entities are behind these attacks. At midnight, many deadly things are crawling, moving, and flying.

It is time to dominate your environment, it is time to dominate your spiritual atmosphere. It is time you rose up and take dominion in your life as your spiritual mandate given to you by God.

Arise and engage in midnight prayer if you want sure success and victory at every point in your life and destiny.

Scriptural references

- **1 Thessalonians 5:17 –**

  Pray without ceasing.

- **1 Timothy 2:1-4 –**

  I exhort therefore, that, first of all, supplications, prayers, intercessions, and giving of thanks, be made for all men

- **Jeremiah 33:3 –**

  Call unto me, and I will answer thee, and shew thee great and mighty things, which thou knowest not.

- **Ephesians 6:18 –**

Praying always with all prayer and supplication in the Spirit, and watching thereunto with all perseverance and supplication for all saints;

- **Psalms 34:17 –**

The righteous cry, and the LORD heareth, and delivereth them out of all their troubles.

- **Acts 16:25 – 26,**

"And at midnight Paul and Silas prayed, and sang praises unto God: and the prisoners heard them. And suddenly there was a

great earthquake, so that the foundations

of the prison were shaken: and immediately

all the doors were opened, and every one's

bands were loosed."

- Exodus 12:29-30,

  "And it came to pass, that at midnight the

  Lord smote all the firstborn in the land of

  Egypt, from the firstborn of Pharaoh that

  sat on his throne unto the firstborn of the

  captive that was in the dungeon; and all the

  firstborn of cattle. And Pharaoh rose up in

  the night, he, and all his servants, and all

the Egyptians; and there was a great cry in

Egypt; for there was not a house where

there was not one dead."

Made in the USA
Columbia, SC
08 December 2022

73110516R00020